Barack Obama, The Audacity of Being a Global President

Barack Obama, The Audacity of Being a Global President

Philip Ephraim

To order additional copies of this book, contact:
Xlibris Corporation
1-888-795-4274
www.Xlibris.com
Orders@Xlibris.com
52051

CONTENTS

Preface

Millions of people around the globe are hoping that Senator Barack Obama will emerge as the 44th President of United States. President Obama is expected to develop a more positive role for America in the world.

All around the world an energetic and unprecedented movement is growing to ensure Senator Obama's victory at the November general elections. From Germany to Africa, from France to the Caribbean flurries of pro-Obama campaign activities are going on. Even "enemy" of the US like Fidel Castro have called Obama "the most progressive candidate to the U.S. presidency". Examples of the worldwide movement include: In China a dramatic Obama rally is being planned on the Great Wall. In Gaza, a Palestinian student has been making hundreds of campaign phone calls to US over the internet, whenever he has electricity and is not under Israeli bombardment. In Kenya, Obama is so popular that a beer has been named after him! On the internet there over 40 international Obama fan groups on Facebook, many with more than 500 members, focused on Denmark, France, Indonesia, Tanzania and many other countries. There are also dozens of blogs and websites.

In Trinidad, calypso legend, The Mighty Sparrow sings "Barack the Magnificent", and in Jamaica reggae star, Cocoa Tea sings "We Want Obama". In Egypt a humanitarian worker has written letters to dozens of superdelegates urging them to back Obama. And wherever opinion polls have been conducted, comparing him with Senator John McCain, Senator Obama is consistently the favorite candidate by a wide margin, for example:

74% in Japan
71% in Brazil
68% in Holland
64% in South Africa
61% in Britain
54% in Iraq
48% in Switzerland
(Source: *http://www.theworldwantsobama.org/2008_03_01_archive.html*)

On an interconnected and interdependent planet, the policies of the US have a huge impact on every nation on earth. After the long and arrogant Bush years, Senator Obama looks different, he sounds different and millions of non-Americans believe he will behave differently towards them. They may not agree with all his current policies, and they understand that he will face difficult choices and compromises when in office. However, they trust him to do his best because he has demonstrated strong principles and a willingness to listen and engage constructively, even with countries that have been seen as America's enemies.

Chapter 1

Why does the world want Obama to be the US President?

Barack Obama is a "once-in-a-generation leader who connects with the hopes and dreams of the American people and will deliver the long-overdue change that our country desperately needs."
—Harry Reid, Senate Majority Leader.

"You are a once-in-a-lifetime leader," the governor said from the stage. "Above all, you will be a president who brings this nation together."
—Bill Richardson, The New Mexico governor, Former Democratic Presidential Candidate.

When, I wondered, was the last time this country was guided by such a leader? Someone whose moral center was un-embargoed? Someone with courage instead of mere ambition? Someone who truly thinks of his country's citizens as "we," not "they"? Someone who understands what it will take to help America realize the virtues it fancies about itself, what it desperately needs to become in the world?
—Toni Morrison, Legendary Novelist and Nobel Laureate

. . . .

[Most of the materials are from the contents of the world wants Obama website, used by permission.]

1.1   Why Should the World Care About Who Becomes President of the United States?

Why does the world want Obama to be the US President? The global community is increasingly interdependent, and the next US President will make decisions that affect us all. Whether you live in Baghdad, Buenos Aires or Bangkok, it wouldn't matter. So global interest is this process matters.

The World Wants Obama Coalition (1) states, "Although Americans have done many positive things around the world, the US government—once the champion of anti-colonialism and self-determination—has often appeared to be an arrogant bully, waging war and pursuing its own interests at the expense of others. President Bush has taken this to extremes, but the general policy was little better under his predecessors; for example, Bill Clinton imposed economic sanctions on Iraq for all eight years of his presidency, against the wishes of the vast majority of UN countries, causing the unnecessary deaths of hundreds of thousands of Iraqi children.

Senator Obama looks different, he sounds different, and millions of non-Americans believe he will act differently. We cannot vote in the 2008 US elections, but if we could, we'd back Obama. We may not agree with all his current policies, and we understand that he will face difficult choices and compromises when he is in office. However, we trust he will do his best, because he has demonstrated strong principles and a willingness to listen and engage constructively, even with countries that have been seen as America's enemies.

We want an America that lives up to the principles it preaches, listens rather than lectures, conserves rather than consumes, makes peace rather than war and uses its influence positively in the world. This is why the world is interested in US elections".

Barack Obama by his cooperative style of leadership, is the most suited presidential candidate for dealing with new global challenges. These are: defeating discrimination, poverty, shelter and refugee problem, scourge of AIDS, human rights, terror and the well of extremism that supports it, saving this planet by reducing the carbon we send into our atmosphere, building on the wealth that open markets have created, and share its benefits more equitably, securing all loose nuclear materials and stopping the spread of nuclear weapons.

This is the moment to begin the work of seeking the peace of a world without nuclear weapons. Our dividing walls needs to be torn down and we build true partnership and share the burdens of development and diplomacy, of progress and peace. This require allies who will listen to each other, learn from each other and, most of all, trust each other.

We're not saying Obama is perfect, but he is the first Presidential candidate in a long time who seems genuinely willing to listen to the world and take courageous action to work towards a just, peaceful, and sustainable planet—which will be good for Americans and the rest of us. With that kind of President in the White House, Americans will be able to hold their heads up high when they visit other countries and won't need to pretend they are Canadians!"

So there is a global movement out there to show America that there are millions of people around the globe that back Obama, and encourage America to engage international opinion. They are not affiliated with the Obama Campaign, but are an independent network of global citizens.

Barack Obama earned his law degree from Harvard in 1991, where he became the first African-American president of the Harvard Law Review. Finally, his advocacy work led him to run for the Illinois State Senate, where he served for eight years. In 2004, he became the third African American since Reconstruction to be elected to the U.S. Senate.

Whether it's the poverty exposed by Katrina, the genocide in Darfur, or the role of faith in our politics, Barack Obama continues to speak out on the issues that will define America in the 21st century.

1.2   Global Issues Obama Discusses:

i.   Talk to Foes and Friends:

Obama is willing to meet with the leaders of all nations, friend and foe. And if America is willing to come to the table, the world will be more willing to rally behind American leadership to deal with challenges like terrorism, Iran and nuclear programs.

ii.   Expand Diplomatic Presence:

To make diplomacy a priority, Obama will stop shutting down consulates and start opening them in the tough and hopeless corners of the world—particularly in Africa. He will expand foreign service, and develop the capacity of civilian aid workers to work alongside the military.

iii. Fight Global Poverty:

Obama will double foreign assistance to $50 billion. He will help the world's weakest states to build healthy and educated communities, reduce poverty, develop markets, and generate wealth **(2)**.

iv.   Obama is better positioned to deal with issues like . . .

   Genocide In Darfur
   War in Iraq and Afghanistan
   Africa—HIV/AIDS, Poverty and War
   Climate Change
   Iran and Nuclear Weapons
   Israel and Palestine . . . and much more.

v.   The world is one global village.

As members of the WORLD, we share the same experiences. We share a common humanity and the world is one global village.

Obama underscored the inter-connectedness of the people of the world in his celebrated speech in Berlin on "July 24, 2008. "The terrorists of September 11th plotted in Hamburg and trained in Kandahar and Karachi before killing thousands from all over the globe on American soil.

As we speak, cars in Boston and factories in Beijing are melting the ice caps in the Arctic, shrinking coastlines in the Atlantic, and bringing drought to farms from Kansas to Kenya.

Poorly secured nuclear material in the former Soviet Union, or secrets from a scientist in Pakistan could help build a bomb that detonates in Paris. The poppies in Afghanistan become the heroin in Berlin. The poverty and violence in Somalia breeds the terror of tomorrow. The genocide in Darfur shames the conscience of us all.

In this new world, such dangerous currents have swept along faster than our efforts to contain them. That is why we cannot afford to be divided. No one nation, no matter how large or powerful, can defeat such challenges alone"

1.3 Obama Knows Our World.

Obama has a worldwide family. There is a significance of Obama's family being spread around the world: "Obama's bridge-building instincts come from somewhere. They are rooted and proven. For an expectant and often alienated world, they are of central significance. Obama's half-sister Auma has been quoted as saying: My daughter's father is British. My mom's brother is married to a Russian. I have a brother in China engaged to a Chinese woman". This adds to the familiar Obama story spanning Hawaii, Kenya and Indonesia. With more than seven million people naturalized in the past decade, it's harder to separate America's fate from that of others. Isolationism is not merely wrong, it's impossible. If elected, Obama would be the first genuinely 21st-century leader. The China-Indonesia-Kenya-Britain-Hawaii web mirrors a world in flux.

1.4 Obama Can Transform the World's Image of America.

This is view shared by Diane Abbott British MP, for Hackney North in London, who said. "That moment on a freezing January day in Washington when a black man and his family stand on the steps of the Capitol to take the presidential oath will be flashed up all over the world. The wordless message to young black people from New York to Nairobi, Johannesburg to Brixton will be of a whole new world of personal possibilities. America's sense of itself will be redeemed. The way that the world sees it will be transformed." (3) Obama will change the present negative American image. This is not who we are! Hear Andrew Sullivan (4) "Obama brings something no one else does to this moment. By replacing one of the most globally despised and domestically divisive presidents in American history with a young leader half-Kansan and half-Kenyan, America would be saying something to the world: Bush-Cheney is not who we are. America is not what it has come to appear to be. This country is among the most culturally and racially and religiously diverse on the planet. America has long been a powerful and vital beacon for human rights—not, as recently, the avatar of torture, rendition and executive tyranny."

1.5   A Journalist's Experience Abroad.

Byron York a **(5)** White House correspondent for National Review was recently in Paris. Let me start with a story he shared with us in his article, Obama for president of the world. I'm having lunch with an Obama supporter at La Coupole, the venerable brasserie in Paris's Montparnasse neighborhood. A woman came along with her fiancé to discuss something else, but the talk inevitably comes round to the U.S. presidential race. And the question here, as all across Europe, is:

What reason could there possibly be for Barack Obama not to be the next president of the United States?

Put another way, why would anyone vote for John McCain?

There are any number of reasons I could mention, but since we had just gotten word in the last few hours of the Supreme Court's decision in the Boumediene case, in which the narrowest possible majority, 5-4, voted that prisoners in Guantanamo Bay can go to federal court to challenge the U.S. government's right to detain them, I bring up the issue of judges.

A decision like Boumediene is bad enough from the current court, I say. If Obama were elected, it would certainly get worse.

My lunch companion doesn't agree. In the European mind, Guantanamo is one of the centers of evil in the world, a dungeon where George W. Bush commits unspeakable acts on innocent Muslims who just happened to be on a battlefield in Afghanistan or Pakistan when U.S. troops captured them.

She says the prisoners in Gitmo have been denied their constitutional rights.

I say they are enemy combatants; they have rights under international treaties, but not American constitutional rights.

But they have "global rights," she insists.

What are "global rights"? I ask.

There's no precise definition, but as far as I could tell, "global rights" appear to be American constitutional rights applied to the entire planet. It's an astounding notion, given that American constitutional rights definitely do not apply across the entire planet—not even in places like, well, France.

Do you have global rights? I ask. What if you make some public statement offensive to Muslims? Here in France, you might be prosecuted. Do you have a "global right" to freedom of speech or not?

Is there a "global" First Amendment?

We went round and round without reaching any agreement on much of anything. And then things went downhill a little further when the talk turned to the subject of Obama and race. She told me that in France there isn't the racial segregation one finds in the United States.

I had to wonder about that. I saw almost no black faces around us in Montparnasse, but the day before, in a part of Montmartre, I saw almost all black faces.

And what about those almost entirely minority suburbs on the outskirts of Paris? Could it be that there are residential divisions of racial, ethnic and religious groups—nothing dictated by law, just residential patterns—in France, too? Is it segregation in the U.S. but something else here?

And what about politics? An article in The New York Times a few days ago discussed how there is "one black member representing continental France in the National Assembly among 555 members; no continental French senators out of some 300; only a handful of mayors out of some 36,000, and none from the poor Paris suburbs."

So here in France they are very, very excited about Barack Obama, but have made it somewhat unlikely that an Obama of their own will emerge.

I have a friend in London, very Euro in outlook, who is terrifically frustrated and worried about the election.

His chief concern: the role of Americans. "It's a pity that Americans are the ones who elect the president," he says. "It would be much better if the people of the world voted on the American president."

And guess who would be elected in such a scenario? Here's a hint: It's not John McCain.

But alas, our system works differently. We're going to have a campaign, and then Americans will decide who will be president.

Whether Obama wins or loses, he will still be a hero here in France.

Just as long as he doesn't try to run for office.

Senator Barack Obama has been described as a once in a life time Leader. The Blog, Why we Need Obama, discusses the principle of a catalytic leader and his role in the world. Some to absurdly confuse catalytic leader with a cult leader. In a post titled Obama: A Profoundly Catalytic Leader, the blog notes: "I think many Americans and the media are struggling with how to most accurately understand Senator Obama's popularity and leadership style. We have a responsibility to help expand their understanding and give them new concepts to explain why Senator Obama is and will be so profoundly effective".

What then is a catalytic leadership style? This is the exact style of leadership our country and our interconnected world requires at this point in history. Without this more accurate framing, the media will continue to parrot Senator Clinton's talking points by attributing Senator Obama's message and popularity to hero worship, charisma, blind faith or "cultmania", etc.

Catalytic Leadership is a style of leadership whereby a leader inspires diverse constituencies to step forward and work together and where effective solutions to problems are created by such constituencies working together, with everyone buying into the problem solving process. By being involved and invested in the process, stakeholders who may desire different outcomes may yet come to support a solution because they were made a part of the process. They can say "WE DID IT!"

Senator Obama is clearly a charismatic figure. However, to write him off as simply a "charismatic figure" is too simplistic. His true power lies in what appears to be his natural leadership ability and his skill at drawing together a variety of diverse constituencies into his decision-making process. Not everyone will agree with the outcome of every initiative he puts forward but everyone will at least be able to say that they were consulted and had their voices heard. Thus, his message of "Yes WE can!".

The complexity of the problems facing our country and world involve highly divergent points of view and diverse people/communities that must somehow find common ground in order to move toward solutions, and a Catalytic Leadership style is the one that is necessary. This is one of the critically important skills that Senator Barack Obama will bring to the presidency, as is already profoundly evidenced in his ongoing campaign.

A Catalytic Leader is the antidote to our current woes and the media's recent "cultmania" spin in answer to Obama's popularity and his ability to inspire and involve so many patriotic Americans—whether Democrat, Independent or Republican.

We cannot suffer through another era where "leadership" is defined as forcing your will upon others, not consulting with opposing voices and falling prey to the supposed collective wisdom of a coterie that has never disagreed with you.

America needs to repair her image in the world. Obama may be the messenger to get this done. In an article titled, The Global Obama, Andrew Sullivan, back from vacation, make a compelling case as follows "The simple existence of Obama as a new president in a new century would in itself enhance America's soft power immeasurably, just as a clear decision to leave Iraq would provide much greater leverage for diplomacy and military force in a whole variety of new ways. Obama would mean the rebranding of America, after a disastrous eight years(6)"

Chapter 2

Is Obama popular globally?

Obama would be elected in November. "When that happens, it will change everything. You'll have to measure time by 'Before Obama' and 'After Obama,' It's an exciting time to be alive now." Every thing's going to be affected by this seismic change in the universe,"

—Spike Lee, American Film Director.

"Yes we can. If we stand together, to build . . . One America, that rebuilds its moral authority in the world. The war in Iraq will end in 2009 . . . when Barack Obama is president of the United States of America."

—John Edwards, US Senator,
Former Democratic presidential candidate.

Obama "offers hope" to the world. He wrote the song, "YES WE CAN."

—Will.i.am—The Black Eyed Peas producer.

. . . .

2.1 International Appeal

To the question of whether Obama has an international appeal, the answer is yes, a great deal. In an extraordinary appearance in Berlin on Thursday July 24th, 2008, Obama delivered a substantive address on the pointy-headed subject of trans-Atlantic relations. The police estimated that over 200,000 people—perhaps the largest live audience that Mr Obama has ever addressed—thronged the boulevard that stretches between the Prussian Victory Column and the Brandenburg Gate. This was one of the stops Senator Obama made in his week-long trip which took him through the Middle East and Europe, starting with Afghanistan, Iraq, Jordan, Israel and the West Bank and finishing with Germany, France and Britain. This international debut was designed to deepen his foreign policy credentials, and signal the possibility of a new era in U.S. relations with the rest of the world and test his popularity abroad. What Obama demonstrated in the Middle East, and in Europe, is that, whatever his opponents say and have said about his inexperience, he is politically a man of the world. He is not only smart—we all knew that—but he listens to other people and actually seems to care about what they think and want in this new world.

(i) The Statistics: Indicator of International Enthusiasm for Senator Obama (The Three Minutes Test!)

These days if you Google for "X for Obama" where "X" can be the name of pretty much any country or people group, you'll find that there is at least one, and sometimes many, spontaneous initiatives at community organizing in support of his Presidential bid. Try the same test with Clinton or McCain and you almost certainly won't find anything (though there were a few of international support groups for Ron Paul). This fact, perhaps more than all the opinion polls and articles that back it up, is proof that Senator Obama has a global appeal that goes far beyond any other Presidential candidate. Former U.S. President Jimmy Carter says he's found strong support for Barack Obama during his recent trips to Africa and Asia. Carter says Obama was the favorite in his travels to Ghana, Nigeria and Nepal. He says "world opinion is strongly supportive of Obama, that's all we hear".

(ii) International Polls: Online and Offline Polls of Many Countries Demonstrate Obama's Global Appeal.

An international research organization, IPSOS (7) polled 22,605 people across 22 countries, thus representing one of the largest international poll conducted so far on the issue. The questions were designed as part of IPSOS's bi-annual Global Advisor-Reputation Risk Identifier survey, and carried out between April 15 and May 22, 2008. Senator Obama was the overall favorite; 55%

of people who were aware of all three candidates expressed support for him (compared to 31% for Senator Clinton and 14% for John McCain). He was also individually the favorite in each of the 22 countries surveyed (his backing ranged from 42% in India to 71% in Argentina). Clinton was unsurprisingly the most well known (recognized by 92% of those polled), given that she has been in the public eye since the early 90s. Obama was not far behind in recognition (82%), with McCain trailing somewhat on the international stage (62%). The poll also demonstrated the depth of global interest in the elections, with 80% of respondents who were aware of all three candidates saying that they were following the elections closely.

(iii) Global Voting Websites

A couple of websites have been set up independently to try and assess world opinion on the US elections. What if we all voted? has received 922 votes so far from people in 57 countries, resulting in 48% for Obama, 23% for Clinton, 9% for McCain and the balance for candidates who have dropped out (Ron Paul got an impressive 14%). Ron Paul's dedicated online campaigners meant he also did well on another site, Who Would the World Elect, which received over 38,000 international votes; out of the three main candidates Obama received 72% of the vote, McCain 4%. Al-Jazeera International has received about 10,000 votes so far on its website, with Obama in the lead with 76% of the votes cast for the main three candidates (Clinton 15%, McCain 9%).

The Global Vote Project has a similar vision, although it is going to be focusing on the main event—the Presidential elections—and not the primaries (BetaVote did this in 2004 with Kerry receiving 88% of nearly half a million votes)

VoteMatch USA 2008 is an initiative of the Dutch Institute for Political Participation which asks you to choose between Obama's and Clinton's policies on 13 issues (Iraq, Cuba, immigration etc.), which you can also weigh in based on which issues they consider most important. The result is a score showing which of the two most closely matches your views. It's a good idea, although most of the issues are not foreign policy, and some (like disparity in sentencing between cocaine and crack) are a bit esoteric for most non-Americans to have formed a view about. The results at present show 68% for Obama out of 23,018 votes cast on the Dutch version of the site, and

70% for Obama out of 1102 votes cast on the English version, since 20th February. There are a number of similar US-based candidate match websites, e.g. VoteHelp, VAJoe, PriceGrabber and USA Today—all of these should be taken with a pinch of salt, as the questions posed and the specific working of the possible answer can obviously skew the results. The Dutch version has an advantage over the others in that it focuses on the two remaining Democrat candidates and uses their specific quotes rather an a third-party assessment of their policy stances.

Voices Without Votes is a phenomenal site created by the Global Voices blogging network, with support from Reuters, which aggregates posts about the US elections of hundreds of bloggers around the world. Though none of these sites can give a fully representative picture of global opinion, but they can provide pieces of the jigsaw when combined with other kinds of polls.

Here are the results from polls conducted by The WorldWantsObama.org (8) of 1000 people across 5 countries in Africa, Asia, Europe, Middle East and Latin America:

71% of Brazilians support Obama, (McCain 15%)
61% of Londoners (UK) support Obama, (McCain 7%)
54% of Iraqis support Obama, (McCain 21%)
74% of Japanese support Obama, (McCain 9%)
64% of South Africans support Obama, (McCain 12%)

The polls were conducted from February 16th-February 23rd (using Facebook polls—http://www.facebook.com/business/?polls), the sample size was 200 For Each Poll, targetted at specific national networks (London was used because there is no Facebook network for the UK as a whole). The question asked was "Non-Americans, who should be the next US president?" The order of the candidates was automatically randomized so there would be no bias towards Senator Obama.

(iv) In Britain

Ahead of Senator Obama's planned visit to Britain in a few weeks, a new a Guardian/ICM poll (9) shows that 53% of Britons believe that Senator Obama would make the better president, with only 11% favoring McCain

(36% declined to express an opinion). These results confirm numerous poll results during the primaries which showed that the proverbial 51st state have favored Obama since early in the electoral race, with the margins in his favor increasing as Britons have learn more about him. The strength of the result may also seem surprising given that the governing Labor Party of Gordon Brown, which is ideologically closer to the US Democrats, is extremely unpopular and the opposition Conservative party is polling its greatest lead since the times of Margaret Thatcher. Previous polls broken down by political affiliation have also confirmed that Obama leads among Conservatives in Britain.

The UK Telegraph's poll **(10)** has revealed Obama is particularly popular in Italy, where 70% of respondents said they prefer him to McCain. The French were not far behind, with 65 % saying they would back Obama. In Germany, 67% of respondents gave the Democratic candidate the nod, while only 6 % backed McCain. In the week of his visit to Germany, A Pew Research Centre poll showed Germans favoured Obama over McCain by a 49 point margin. Influential weekly Der Spiegel dedicated its weekend issue to the visit, putting a picture of Obama on the cover and the title "Germany meets the Superstar"

(v) From English, Baby! Website, Students Swing to Obama.

Obama has repeatedly topped online and offline polls, many of which we've profiled before. Some interesting new data comes from English, Baby!, the most visited website for English language students with 750,000 members. It has run a series of polls related to the US Presidential elections. The first, in June 2007, gave Senator Clinton a 32% lead over the other candidates. However a second poll, in April 2008, showed a dramatic shift to Senator Obama, who finished 20% ahead after 4345 votes were cast. He is even further ahead in their third, and ongoing, poll: at the moment he leads at 61%, compared to 31% for Senator Clinton and 8% for John McCain. English, baby! co-founder, John Hayden explains: "It's been interesting to watch opinion change. The Clinton name has been very recognizable throughout the world but Obama's message seems to be taking hold." **(11)** On the website's forums, individual members can be observed changing their opinions. Hakimi, a 32-year-old user from Yemen started a forum thread about Hillary Clinton. But last January, he was won over by Obama. "This morning I heard Barack

Obama speaking about the results in New Hampshire . . . He has the potential to be an incredible leader that could do truly amazing things . . ." English, Baby! aims to teach English in an innovative MTV-style, virtually immersing students in American culture and conversational English.

(vi) Brazilian Blog for Obama

A few months ago Brazil topped a Facebook polls, with 71% of Brazilians backing Obama. Now a Brazilian, Miguel Leonel dos Santos, has started a blog about the election at: BarackObamaPresidente.blogspot.com, Miguel writes: "Barack Obama is the hope for change in the U.S., and will not only promote friendly relations with people around the world, but also improve the economic conditions of the American people. As Obama said, "the time for change has come" and we have faith in the words of this Senator who has wonderful ideas and powerful ideals." There's a YouTube clip of Miguel and friends cheering for Obama in a typically exuberant Brazilian way.

(vii) Swiss Prefer Obama

If the Swiss could take part and cast a vote in the US presidential race, they would clearly vote for Barack Obama. According to a survey launched by the Swiss weekly newspaper L'Hebdo . . . 47.7% **(12)** of people in a Switzerland-wide survey would like to see Obama as the next American President, only 4.9% favour John McCain. The Swiss do not trust him to improve the reputation of the USA. Given that 17.6% of those polled were undecided, out of those who expressed an opinion Obama got 58% of the vote!

(viii) New Zealand

A poll of New Zealanders asking who they would like to see run against Republican John McCain in the US election revealed 47 % chose Obama, compared to 31 % supporting Hillary Clinton. A further 22 per cent were unable to offer an opinion. The telephone survey involved 750 people aged 18 and over, interviewed between April 24 and May 1 . . . The poll found National and Labor voters [the more right and left wing parties respectively] recorded almost identical results with National voters preferring Obama 44% to 33% and Labor voters preferring him 47% to 33%.

(ix) From Canada

With the longest undefended international border (5,522 miles long) and as the largest trade partner, what happens in the US matters a great deal up in Canada. A recent Harris-Decima poll (13) suggests Canadians of every age group, political stripe and gender prefer the rookie senator over his adversaries, Democrat Hillary Clinton and Republican nominee John McCain. When asked which of the three candidates they liked most, respondents preferred Obama over McCain by an almost five-to-one margin—39 % to 8 %. Even among self-declared Conservatives, Obama had almost double McCain's support. Obama also had a nine-point edge over Clinton. That is a drastic turnaround from January, when the better-known Clinton had an 11-point lead among Canadian poll respondents . . . When asked who they thought would win the presidency, 44 % said Obama, 19 % said McCain, and only 17 % predicted there would be a second Clinton in the White House . . . The poll of 1,000 Canadians was conducted from April 3 to 6.

Canadians for Obama has been organizing road trips south of the border to volunteer with the Obama campaign. Canadian blogger Daryl Wonk (14) was fortunate enough to be in Chicago on Super Tuesday. He writes "Maybe I was speaking for the majority of Canadians and Conservatives when I shook Obama's hand on Super Tuesday and said "Canada loves you too". There are around a dozen Facebook groups for Canadian supporters, many with more than 200 members and the largest Canadians for Barack Obama has over 2300 members. While Canadian Obama supporters are quite serious about their support, they clearly have a fun side to it.

(x) From Asia

83% of Asian leaders at policy forum back Obama

The Asia Society's Williamsburg Conference (15) connects leaders in Asia-Pacific politics, academia and the media with their US counterparts. It was founded in 1971 by John D. Rockefeller and this year the conference was held in Bali, Indonesia, from 3-6 April. Participants discussed the US elections, and were asked to give one piece of advice to the next US president, and to comment on their preferred candidate. Over 83% of those interviewed expressed a preference for Senator Obama. The Asia-Pacific region contains almost 2/3rds of the world's population and many of the US' most important trading partners. Obama's popularity in this region could be a huge boon to international relations if he is elected President.

2.2 Global Opinions: What the People of the World are Saying

(i) Support for Obama at U.S.-Islamic World Forum

Tamara Cofman Wittes, **(16)** Senior Fellow at the Saban Center for Middle East Policy of the Brookings Institution, blogs about her positive experiences at the 5th U.S.-Islamic World Forum in Qatar: "Quite honestly, though, I don't think the relative love-fest at this year's meeting is all ascribable either to regional shifts or to the conference organizers' choice of speakers. The most powerful explanation for the change is evident in the overwhelming fact that all anyone at this conference really wants to talk about is Barack Obama. A friend from the Gulf tells me her young relative was so excited about the Democratic candidate that he tried to donate money over the Internet, as he'd heard so many young Americans were doing. Then he found out he had to be a U.S. citizen to do so. Another young woman, visiting from next-door Saudi Arabia, said that all her friends in Riyadh are "for Obama." The symbolism of a major American presidential candidate with the middle name of Hussein, who went to elementary school in Indonesia, certainly speaks to Muslims abroad. But more important is just the prospect of a refreshing shift in the breeze off the Potomac. More than the changes in the region, it seems to be anticipated changes in Washington that are drawing the eyes of my Arab counterparts and giving the conference its unusually forward-looking tone."

AFP also reports from the Forum: "Obama . . . won overwhelming support in a mock election by more than 200 American and Muslim delegates at the US-Islamic World Forum in the Qatari capital. The Republican candidates won only a handful of votes." The influential Egyptian Islamic television preacher Amr Khaled told AFP: **(17)** "I would like to see Obama become president of America because he champions 'change and hope', which we Muslims need as much as the Americans do."

(ii) Palestinian Student in Gaza Launches a Campaign to Support Obama

"A Palestinian youth from Gaza is working hard in day and night as a for free volunteer appealing the American citizens to vote for the US presidency democratic candidate Senator Barak Obama. Ibrahim Abu Jayyab, 23, **(18)** living in the besieged Gaza Strip, decided to support Obama in his harsh competition against his competitor Hillary Clinton in the on-going US presidential election campaign. Abu Jayyab, who studies media in Gaza, says that he uses a for-free internet communication software programs to call as much as possible US citizens persuading them to vote for Obama. He spends long hours on internet and watching TV news to follow up any developments on the running elections in the United States. Abu Jayyab tries to realize the state or city where the elections are going to be held, and then he phones people at the same state. "I phone tens or hundreds of random phone numbers calling them to vote for Obama because he is the man of the future," Abu Jayyab told RNA **(19)** reporter. He thinks that if Obama becomes the US President he will help the Palestinians to achieve their dreams. "We cannot achieve our dreams because of the Israeli occupation, the world did not help us to end the Israeli occupation and we hope Obama will achieve what the world could not, by helping us to live in peace and to achieve our dreams."

(iii) Turkey

Opinion: Obama will be good for the Turks—and the world

The Turks feel that Barack Obama can be the leader that the world is looking for. He can put a new list of criteria to judge what is good and bad for American people. He can stop the hate wars between Muslims and Christians by promoting peace and helping communities in need. He can be the one to stop dropping the bombs and start sending doctors, food and clothing as well as capital to create more jobs, to build more hospitals and schools all over the world . . . Turks will not feel friendly to the US as long as they don't feel the America's Iraqi policies are completely changed. And it looks like only Obama can change it . . . The United States needs a completely new President to change her image and to make a difference in the world for the better with her own actions. American politics "as usual" is not going to be enough to give hope to nations of the planet including Turks . . . Barack Obama is . . . good for Turks, as well as the rest of the world." (In the Turkish Daily News, by Vural Cengiz, **(20)** the president of the Turkish-American Businessmen's Union).

(iv) Iran

Iranian blogger says Obama represents a "paradigm shift" in the US's image

Jahanshah Rashidian, an Iranian now living in Germany, writes: **(21)** "If Barack Obama were a candidate in Germany, he would be elected as German President, according to a German newspaper, Wiesbadener Kurier. I would also vote for him . . . The US needs another face, a face less repulsive, less aggressive, and less immoral. For that face, Barack Obama stands for a new hope, more than any other recent President in the US . . . What makes Obama more attractive is his originality: Obama is more intelligent than to be blindly nationalistic, he is more honest than to be a president of Big Companies . . . His first symbolic message to the world is the end of racial discrimination which has been written in the Constitution but not yet in the collective memory of humanity. His second message is to reduce an increasing negative image of the US in the world. Obama's era accelerates this paradigm shift.

Obama cannot radically change the established system of immoral capitalism, but he may incite new values for a humanized system like a better welfare, more social justice and more civil rights . . . I think Obama's intellectual charisma can contribute to break down any extremist ideology, including Islamism. His humanitarian and intellectual influence can trigger a shake-up of Islamist resistance in the world, including in the Muslim societies. Obama's era will go beyond religious and racial divisions of people—divisions created by unwritten constitutions of white societies and the three decades of Islamism, reborn in Iran. The time has come that people look for other criteria to catalogue people, rather than by race or religion."

(v) Iraq

One Iraqi working for the UN wrote: "I prefer him for the sake of change—hopefully he will be able to do something. Iraqi politicans need to be urged too much to work and get results".

(vi) Singapore (Asia)

Asian diplomat says Obama's victory would have dramatic global implications

Kishore Mahbubani, dean of Singapore's Lee Kuan Yew School of Public Policy and former Ambassador and President of the UN Security Council, writes in a Newsweek **(22)** article, If The World Could Vote: "It is clear whose election would have the most dramatic effect: Barack Obama's. In one fell swoop, an Obama victory would eliminate at least half the massive anti-Americanism now felt around the world. Eight hundred million Africans would get a tremendous boost to their self-esteem and cultural pride. A son of their soil would, for the first time, occupy the White House, and many would whisper, approvingly, 'Only in America.'"

Obama is not a Muslim, but the 1.2 billion Muslims around the world would take great interest in his middle name: Hussein. Indeed, the election of "H" would immediately undo much of the damage "W" has wrought. W pushed hard for the democratization of the Islamic world, but H's election would accomplish far more. Young Muslims would quickly start asking why America can elect a young Hussein when their own states are stuck with aging, visionless leaders. Obama has said that "the United States is seen as arrogant and aloof" and that "the world will work with—not against—U.S. power if it is put to principled use and directed towards common goals." Were he to implement this thinking as president, the world would become a safer place.

(vii) Bangladesh

The Guardian—Tahmima Anam

He'll never be my president, but I still found myself campaigning for Obama on a chilly street corner **(23)** talking about "our next president" as though the changes in the system are actually going to affect me. It's not just because the next president of the United States is indeed in some significant way my president—because if he doesn't lower the carbon emissions Bangladesh is going to drown, because if he invades Iran he may invade Bangladesh next, because our currency is pegged to the dollar—but because, somehow, I feel that the death of idealism in this country would mean the death of idealism everywhere in the world. I was born in Bangladesh, but raised in Paris, New York and Bangkok, and I now live in London. I'm not even a US citizen. Nor am I a campaign addict. I have never campaigned for any Bangladeshi candidate. I have never asked anyone for their time, their attention, their vote. But here I am, on the corner of Prospect and Mass Ave, cheering for a man who will never be my president."

(viii) Indonesia

Many Indonesians cheer Obama in Democrat race

Few are more fired up than Indonesians, who can lay claim to Democratic hopeful Barack Obama as nearly one of their own . . . "I prefer Obama because he is from a minority. So far, there is no leader coming from a minority," said Samuel Moeloek, 28, a management graduate at Parahiyangan University in the West Java city of Bandung . . . "I think the president has to be incredibly internationally aware and bring global stability and improve relations and the image of the U.S.," said Richard Mau, a hotel marketing executive based in Jakarta, who is backing Obama. "He needs to think about how the U.S. is perceived. The U.S. is not perceived as well as it could be in this region."(24)

(ix) India

"Obama win could win over the world"—Prof. Nalapat

"Despite their liberal credentials, U.S. foreign policy under the Clintons was marked by an Al Gore paternalism toward societies not of European origin . . . A Clinton presidency would continue policy on a course that separates the world into "the West and the rest," while an Obama presidency—with its symbolism fused to the policy prescriptions of the candidate—would give the United States the opportunity to win over not land space, as during the colonial past, but mind space." (25) Professor M.D. Nalapat is vice-chair of the Manipal Advanced Research Group, UNESCO Peace Chair, and professor of geopolitics at Manipal University.

(x) Nepal

Obama charms and inspires Nepali journalists

Nepali journalist Deepak Adhikari(26) got a surprise this week. He's in the US on secondment to the Pittsburgh Post Gazette, on a break from writing for the Nepal Weekly. When he heard that Senator Obama would be passing through the area, he expected a distant glance at most, but instead Barack dropped by the office and met all of the journalists:

"I was busy working on my training plan which is due Wednesday. I saw colleagues running toward the hallway saying "Obama is meeting personally everyone in the newsroom". For a moment, I thought of staying in my desk. But, as everyone flocked to the place where Obama was, I could not resist.

He was shaking hands and moving toward where I was. As he approached me, I introduced myself. I said: I'm from Nepal. He said: Oh, it's a beautiful country. I said: Nice to meet you. He said: Nice to meet you too. Then, he moved ahead. Now almost every one in the newsroom is talking about how he looked like, how his handshake was, etc. Comments vary from his handshake being soft to he looking young. To me he appeared a guy-next-door, attending to everyone. Back home, politicians are a different tribe; they don't relate to the people. They think that they are superior to the people who elect them. I think part of the reason many of prominent leaders lost the recent election is they are not attached to the common people the way Obama is."

Deepak's journalist friend Dinesh Wagle, back in Kathmandu, has also been blogging about the US elections because: "Even in these chilly days, we drink Coca Cola . . . I am typing these lines on MS Word . . . Nine out of 13 tabs on Firefox . . . display American websites. A paper lies on the floor on my left side that's known around the world as the New York Times . . . America, America everywhere . . . Tired of reading about foreign interference in Nepali politics? Watch out: I will be interfering in the American politics!" Although initially favoring Clinton, he eventually decided to endorse Obama shortly before Super Tuesday because: "What American needs is freshness, cool ideas, and plans that can collectively inspire the rest of the world."

Another Nepali, Ayusha Nirola, who edits "Today's Youth Asia", wants Nepali politicians to emulate Obama's positivity: "I hope that the upcoming generation of young leaders look at Obama as an example of an extraordinary leader. Nepalese politicians need to be clear about what they are fighting for and what changes they want to make and how to get there. At a time when every politician seems to be pointing their fingers at each other, to do a positive campaign would mean to bring about a shift in Nepal's political dynamics. If the leader is determined to bring about a positive change not by doing dirty politics, then this will ultimately shift his attention from him to his people and the country and focus on how to improve our Education, Health system and keep the economy growing. YES WE CAN (change the face of NEPAL for better)."

These are strong sentiments. The chief message it captures in that "Obama is an inspiration not only to Americans but people around the globe. He truly exhibits the qualities of a great leader and this is what America and the world needs . . . a leader and not a politician."

(xi) From Russia

Gorbachev's former foreign policy advisor praises Obama

Evgeny Bazhanov is a leading Russian foreign policy specialist who advised Mikhail Gorbachev during the final years of the USSR, and currently vice president for research at the Russia's Diplomatic Academy. He was asked in an interview which candidate for US presidency would be best for Russia:

He explains that he thinks it is Mr. Obama due to his personal convictions . . . [he] will try to make U.S. foreign policy more reasonable and acceptable to other members of the world community . . . Mrs. Clinton will not be equally innovative but she is also much more preferable to us than Mr. McCain. This man appreciates nothing but sheer force, which Russia can respond only by engaging in a new arms race. And we neither want, need nor can afford that." **(27)** Bazhanov goes on to explain that there is are serious geo-political differences between Russia and the West fueled by historical memories and especially by Washington's attempts to achieve hegemony in international affairs . . . However, there are at the same time opportunities for co-operation between Russia and the West, including its leader, the United States. In the security field the two sides face a wide range of identical threats: terrorism, the spread of nuclear weapons, local conflicts that damage the interests of the entire global community, poverty, social injustice, diseases. These are the root of many global security problems.

"After presenting the question to nearly 50 Russians, the answer is clear: 100% of our not-so-random sampling said Senator Barack Obama is their first choice. Huh? Up is down and down is up, at least if you believe conventional wisdom. Why would the Russians, stereotypically considered to be a racist and conservative nation, pick Senator Obama—the first viable black U.S. presidential candidate, and the one who many Americans agree breaks the traditional U.S. presidential mold on many levels? . . . The reasons are varied. Some of Russia have had great experiences in the U.S., and they genuinely believe that the first-term junior senator from Illinois is a leader who is capable of bringing positive change to America. They like Mr. Obama's goal of withdrawing the troops from Iraq and agree with his health care and education policies. Other Russians are more concerned about Russia, and don't like the anti-Putin rhetoric of Senators John McCain. (It is important to remember that Vladimir Putin still enjoys nearly 80 percent approval rating, and most

Russians view themselves as enjoying more freedom and wealth today than ever before in their country's thousand-year history.) John McCain's "I looked into his eyes, and I saw K-G-B," isn't helpful and don't play well with Russians who think seriously about the future of the U.S.-Russia relationship." **(28)**

(xii) Europe

Obama Takes Europe by Storm and Europe Can't Get Enough "Obamamania!

Obama's popularity has soared in Europe since his startling win in Iowa, with European newspapers and television networks from Stockholm to Berlin to London now filled with images of the Illinois senator. In Paris, stories about Obama replaced President Nicolas Sarkozy's love life on the front pages of the newspapers Le Figaro, Libération and Le Monde, **(29)** which on the day after the Iowa caucuses proclaimed: "The Greater America opts for the New Man."

Obama's popularity soars in Germany. Described as the "The New Kennedy." Obama's newfound popularity among Germans underscores not only the breadth of his appeal but also the opportunity he might have as president . . . to mend fences abroad as well as at home.

Mr. Obama has been featured on the cover of the weekly French newsmagazine L'Express, with the headline, "Qui est Barack Obama?" (Who is Barack Obama?) **(30)** The story described him as the Michael Jordan of politics, the prodigy from Chicago, and asked, "Is he the black J.F.K.?" He has also been on the cover of several other best-selling French newsmagazines . . . In France, said Mr. Herbert, Mr. Obama is seen as "being one of us, a foreigner. They don't just see a black candidate; they see him as being able to identify with the outside world, as someone who understands how Europeans and the rest of the world view America, as being able to bridge that gap."

Mr. Obama has also succeeded in seducing the Italians, according to Christopher P. Winner, the editor and publisher of The American, a monthly magazine based in Rome . . . "The Obama factor is something entirely different with the Italian media," Mr. Winner said. "They've decided that he is the millennial version of J.F.K. Because of his global roots, he is an intrinsically more attractive figure."

Infact, Europeans seem to think that Mr. Obama is such a break from American politics as usual that he is, well, almost European." **(31)**

(xiii) Cuba

AlterNet: "One Major Difference Between Clinton and Obama?
Their Records On Cuba"

With Fidel's resignation, Barack Obama's nuanced and progressive position on Cuba is highlighted and illustrates his commitment to supporting democratic change. "If the Cuban leadership begins opening Cuba to meaningful democratic change, the United States must be prepared to begin taking steps to normalize relations and to ease the embargo of the last five decade," Obama said in a recent statement. This reads more like the differences in Clinton's and Obama's Cuban policy.

(xiv) Mexico

Barack Obama landed the cover of Esquire's Spanish issue in March, and captivated journalist Javier del Pino, who admitted that he was infected by "Obamismo,"**(32)** "the virus that affects everyone." Obamismo has spread throughout Latin America's magazine pages and blogs. Recent visitors to Mexico City would find in bookstores magazines as diverse as the literary supplement, Letras Libres, and GQ Mexico, all of which mentioning Obama's name and offered a unique perspective on his candidacy compared to domestic news.

As del Pino concluded, there's passionate interest abroad in Obama, a candidate who is viewed by many as someone who could restore America's image before the rest of the world. Apparently, change and hope is a message that resonates with Mexicans.

(xv) South Africa

Khaya **(33)** from South Africa gives a very careful view of America's strengths and weakness, concluding that if it elects Barack Obama it will send the message to the world "that America has its mojo back":

(xvi) Uganda

Rechtenwald writes about Bernard Sabiti, 25,**(34)** who hosts a radio show combating HIV/AIDS and recently started a Ugandans for Obama (UFO) group. Sabiti says: "We admire his honesty; that is a rare thing in a politician. I placed a few posters around the university asking if people are interested in the election, or if they simply admire him, they should send me an e-mail." He had more than a hundred responses.

Mawa Haruna, 24, adds: "It is not just those in the universities, or those in business who are following the election. If you go to St. Balikuddembe, the main market in Kampala you will find many people who have never set their eyes on a blackboard, who cannot read a newspaper, but they can tell you who Barack Obama is. If he is elected then we feel that more attention will be paid to the problems of Africa."

Another articles mentions The Obama Solidarity Group, another which was launched by students at Makerere University, the largest in Uganda, on January 18. One of the founders, Silver Mulindwa, said: "Our group has been formed to see that our candidate gets support from not only Americans but other parts of the world including Uganda because he is a symbol of Africa in a western democracy. We have campaigned among the Americans working in Uganda and they have shown support for the candidate." The Kampala Monitor also has an article about this phenomenon: Obama bug bites Ugandans.

(xvii) Controversial Egyptian Singer Backs Obama

Obama's latest fan is Shaaban "Shaabolla" Abdel Rahim, a controversial Egyptian pop star who rose to fame with the song "I Hate Israel, but I love Amr Mousa" and has had subsequent hits on themes such as 9/11, the invasion of Iraq and the Mohammed cartoons. He is currently recording a new song "Bye-Bye Bush" in which he says good riddance to the current President and expresses his hope that Senator Obama will succeed, because he is "a good and kindhearted man"**(35).**

Although Obama may not welcome this endorsement, as he would disagree with many of the views Shaabolla has expressed in his songs, it is nonetheless significant. If even such a fierce critic of US policies can be won over, there is a real hope that a President Obama could defuse the hostility to America that has developed in many countries during the Bush years and build a more positive relationship with the Muslim world.

(xviii) In Israel

"The Name of another America is Obama"—Uri Avnery **(36)**

Veteran Israeli peace activist Uri Avnery, a former paramilitary and Knesset Member who founded Gush Shalom (the "Peace Bloc"), a sincere realist, he wrestles with doubts, but finds Senator Obama's courage and optimism compelling. His article "Two Americas" is well worth reading in full. Here are excerpts:

"The decisions of the President of the United States affect every human being on this planet. Unfortunately, the citizens of the world have no part in these elections. But they may, at least, voice an opinion. Availing myself of this right I say: I am for Barack Obama . . . My friend Afif Safieh, now the chief PLO representative in the US, argues that there are two Americas: the America which exterminated the Native Americans and enslaved the blacks, the America of Hiroshima and McCarthy, and the other America, the America of the Declaration of Independence, of Lincoln, Wilson and Roosevelt. In these terms, George Bush belongs to the first. Obama, his opposite in almost every respect, represents the second . . . Hillary is a run of the mill politician. If McCain is a continuation of Bush, Hillary is an extension of the entire present American political system, the present policy and the present routine. But the world needs another America. The name of another America is Obama . . . The great message of Obama is Obama himself. A person who has roots in three continents (and another half: Hawaii). A person whose education spans the wide world. A person who can see reality from the viewpoints of America, Africa and Asia. A person who is both black and white. A new kind of American, an American of the 21st Century."

"I am not as naïve as I sound. I realize that in his speeches there is more enthusiasm than content. We can't know what he will do once elected president. President Obama may disappoint us. But I prefer to take a risk with a man like this than to know in advance what the two routine politicians, his competitors, will do. I am not overly impressed by election speeches. I have conducted four election campaigns myself and I know that there are things one has to say and things one must not say. It's all with limited liability. But beyond all the speechifying, one fact is more important than a million words: Obama opposed the Iraq invasion from the start, when this took integrity and a lot of courage . . . We in Israel know the huge difference between opposing a war in its first, decisive hour, and opposing it after a month, a year or five years."

"It must be asked: Is it good for Israel? All three candidates have groveled at the feet of AIPAC . . . But I know that they have no choice. That's how it is in the USA. In spite of this, Obama succeeded in getting out one courageous sentence. Speaking before a mainly Jewish audience in Cleveland, he said: "There is a strain within the pro-Israel community that says unless you adopt an unwavering pro-Likud approach to Israel, you're anti-Israel and that can't be the measure of our friendship with Israel." I hope that the American Barack (blessed, in Arabic), if elected, will not turn into a replica of the Israeli Barak (lightning, in Hebrew). Real friendship means: when you see that your friend is drunk, you don't encourage him to drive. You offer to take him home. I am longing for an American president who will have the courage and the honesty to tell our leaders: Dear friends, you are drunk with power! You are speeding along a highway that leads to an abyss! Perhaps Barack Obama will be such a friend. This would be a blessing for us, too."

(xix) In France

La France Avec Obama!

The French haven't been so excited about America since they shipped over the Statue of Liberty. Samuel Sovit, the chairman of the Comité Français de Soutien à Barack Obama ("The french support committee for Barack Obama") whose website is http://Pour-Obama.fr (Google translated to English) has written to The World Wants Obama Coalition to explain the situation in France.

He writes that, for the French, "Obama gives America a human face again. His political program is consistent, pragmatic and effective and his foreign policy is internationalist rather than being based on the concept of a fortress America as the world's policeman." He explains that: "The French polls are all favorable to Barack Obama (e.g. Liberation, CSA), ranking him ahead of Senator Clinton even though his level of recognition was significantly lower [N.B. the last polls were conducted before Super Tuesday, and one expects that his ratings will be even better if new polls were conducted now]. But the most remarkable thing is the level of mobilization behind him here in France, and he is the only candidate who has prompted such enthusiasm."(**37**)

The Committee has already gathered the support of many eminent French politicians, on both the left and the right, particularly those with an interest in foreign affairs. Some notable examples are:

Axel Poniatowski MP—Chairman of the Foreign Affairs Committee and Chairman of the French-US Friendship Committee.

Renaud Muselier MP—Vice-chairman of the Foreign Affairs Committee and former Secretary of State for Foreign Affairs (2002-5)

Pierre Lellouche MP—former President of NATO's Parliamentary Assembly

Jack Lang MP—Former Secretary of Education

Bertrand Delanoé—Mayor of Paris and potential candidate for the Presidency in 2012.

Other Members of Parliament who support him include: Charles de Courson, Marie-George Buffet, Dominique Bussereau, Nathalie Kosciusko-Morizet, Martine Aubry, Claude Goasguen, Yves Jégo, Louis Giscard d'Estaing, Jean-Louis Bianco, Jean-François Copé, Jean Leonett, Maxime Gremetz, Marie-Jo Zimmermann.

Senator Obama also has support from entrepeneurs, intellectuals and artists including:

Pierre Bergé—Co-founder of Yves Saint-Laurent and leading HIV/AIDS campaigner

Bernard Henry Levy—Philosopher and author of "American Vertigo: Traveling America in the Footsteps of Tocqueville."

Sonia Rykiel—Fashion designer

Olivier Duhamel—Leading constitutional lawyer and political scientist.

Françoise Gaillard—One of France's most prominent literary critics.

Frédéric Mittérand—Film-maker.

The French media has printed numerous articles on French opinions about the elections. The majority conclude that there is a French preference for Senator Obama. For example L'Express newspaper ran an article on 11 March titled French Personalities Choose Obama.

For those who speak French, there are some YouTube videos worth watching including a video blog from an Obama Meetup in France, an interview with Olivier Duhamel and an interview with Axel Poniatowski, MP. Also an interview with Constance Borde, a French-American and superdelegate for Democrats Abroad. For more see the Pour Obama Youtube channel. Americans learning French may enjoy Will.i.am's Yes We Can with French subtitles and Obama's Iowa caucus victory speech with French subtitles. The comments on these videos give hundreds of examples of French enthusiasm for Obama.

At his just concluded world tour, during his stop in Paris on, July 25, 2008, the French President *Nicolas Sarkozy* rolled out the red carpet and more for Democratic presidential candidate *Barack Obama* on Friday, offering an effusive embrace that bordered on an endorsement, while a French media throng recorded the arrival of Europe's suddenly favorite American politician. "Sarkozy: 'Obama? C'est mon copain!" ('Obama? He's my buddy!") "My dear Barack Obama," Sarkozy called the senator from Illinois as the two shared a stage normally reserved for heads of state. Obama called Sarkozy "my dear friend, President Sarkozy" and at one point laid a friendly hand on his host's shoulder. This was carried by the liberal journal, Liberation: "OBAMANIA: From Berlin to the suburbs of Lyon, the Democratic candidate who fascinates the world shows the making of a president."**(38)**

(xx) From Opendemocracy

Opendemocracy—"Taking Obama seriously"—Anthony Barnett who initially dismissed Obama, now writes, "It is not just that Obama links the global south to the broken zones of American cities; he also provides a starting-point for an international politics that does not make things worse." Obama's opposition to the war in Iraq proves his character: "Today his stand may seem less distinctive . . . But in the atmosphere of October 2002 everything was at stake: Bush was way high in the polls, an atmosphere of intimidation was building, official patriotism was demanding loyalty in the name of the "war on terror". It was in this context that Obama spoke out and put all his prospects for advancement on the line. What is striking is the quality of his language and the cool—and accurate—assessment of long-term consequence." **(39)**

After Obama clinched the Democratic Nomination, there have been positive reactions to the historic victory. In the aftermath of Obama's victory journalists across the world have been reporting that from Gulf states, South Korea, Asia, Germany, Africa, France to the Caribbean it does seem that the world is supporting Senator Obama's bid to be the next US President. Even an "enemy" of the US like Fidel Castro have called Obama "the most progressive candidate to the U.S. presidency".

The New York Times writes(40) "Across the globe, pundits and politicians of all stripes competed for hyperbole on Wednesday to applaud Senator Barack Obama's claim of victory in the race for the Democratic presidential nomination . . . His triumph in the primaries, many said, signaled the defeat of racism, and if Senator Obama became president, his election would presage a departure from what outsiders have broadly depicted as the go-it-alone belligerence of the Bush era. That anticipatory exuberance cut across party lines."

Chapter 3

Organizing Internationally: Various advocacies of international pro-Obama communities

"He speaks to the America I've envisioned in my music for the past 35 years, a generous nation with a citizenry willing to tackle nuanced and complex problems, a country that's interested in its collective destiny and in the potential of its gathered spirit. He has the depth, the reflectiveness, and the resilience to be our next president,"

—Bruce Springsteen, the Boss, A Rock star.

In addition to keen intelligence, integrity and a rare authenticity, you exhibit something that has nothing to do with age, experience, race or gender and something I don't see in other candidates.

—Toni Morrison, Legendary novelist and Nobel laureate.

"Obama has inspired an enthusiasm and idealism that we have not seen in this country in a long time. Obama speaks with a different voice, a proven agent for change and advocate for middle-class Americans, bringing a new perspective and inspiring a real excitement from the American people."

—Amy Klobuchar, Minnesota Sen.

. . . .

3.1 Organizing Internationally: the Various Global Pro-Obama Communities

How are the international communities globalizing Obama's presidential campaign? There are international communities organizing for barack Obama presidential campaign victory. Below are only representative of what exists.

i.   American Democrats abroad had formed strong campaign groups

    #   Democratsabroad

ii.   There are BarackObama.country groups, such as . . .

    #   BarackObama.ch
    #   BarackObama.fr
    #   BarackObama.ru

iii. There are nationalities4Obama groups, such as . . .

    #   Brits4Obama
    #   Brits for Barack
    #   Brits for Obama
    #   Canadians for Barack Obama
    #   Danes for Obama
    #   Europeans for Barack Obama

iv.   There are Obama-something groups, such as . . .

    #   Libero.it/sognobama
    #   Obama Ohana
    #   Obama.es
    #   Obama4us.net Supporters United!
    #   ObamaInternational
    #   ObamaWorldwide

v.   Immigrant communities in US, such as . . .

    #   Asia-Pacific—Obama Ohana
    #   Asian Americans 4Ob

> \#   Irish Americans 4Ob
> \#   Korean Americans 4Ob
> \#   Latinos—Amigos de Obama
> \#   South Asians 4Ob

vi.   There are country/city for Barack/Obama groups.

> \# Europe, Middle East & Africa Support You.
> \# Canada for Obama
> \# Germany for Obama
> \# Paris for Obama

vii. There Barack Obama international groups, some members in this category
     include . . .

> \#   Barack Obama International Supporters
> \#   Barack Obama (One Million Strong for Barack)
> \#   Barack Obama One World
> \#   Barrack Obama for President
> \#   British Labour party 4 Obama
> \#   Obamaism worldwide
> \#   WeloveBarackObama
> \#   Support! Barack Obama for United States President
> \#   The international community votes for Obama
> \#   The Whole World for Barack Obama
> \#   The World Wants Obama Coalition
> \#   UK for Barak OBAMA 2008
> \#   Americans in Italy for Obama
> \#   ObamaInternational
> \#   ObamaWorldwide(43 members)
> \#   Globamania projects
> \#   Obamaism worldwide

There is a French support group on my.BarackObama.com and also over a
dozen French Facebook groups with a combined membership of over 2000
including:

Groups in France.
France for Barack Obama (596)

Les Socialistes avec Barack Obama! (576)
Pour un ticket Obama / Edwards (416)
J'aimerais trop que Barack Obama soit Président! (140)
Etudiants Français pour Barack Obama (126)
Comité français de soutien à Barack Obama (50)
"The Committee of Friends of Barack Obama."
France endorses Obama (43),
We love Barack Obama too in France (42),
Pour que Barack Obama se présente en France (38),
La France derrière BARACK HUSSEIN OBAMA (32),
Obama appreciation society in France (26),
Barack Obama Fan Club in France (12),
Obama France
Obama President-France Support (12)

3.2   Their Modus Operandi

Naturally, many international supporters of Barack Obama are non Americans. The Obama campaign can't accept foreign donations under the Federal Elections Law. That means every international support group had to sit down and figure out ways of mobilizing a global support that is beyond financial donation. They then had to consider other avenues and activities to apply that support both outside and inside the United States. What then are global groups doing in international organizing for Obama? Below are some of the most **(41)** creative and successful international Barack Obama presidential campaign activities.

(i) Activity One: Subtitling Obama Videos in Many of Worlds' Languages

A phenomenal initiative is underway to produce subtitled Obama videos with captions in many languages. Languages represented so far include Chinese, French, German, Korean, Spanish, Vietnamese. The archive of videos is on YouTube. Some have been optimized for ipods: Visit the website: CaptionedMediaForObama.com. Michael Novak, who is coordinating the translation effort, asks for any members of the World Wants Obama Coalition or readers of the blog who would like to help with translation to get in touch. They particularly want Arabic and Urdu, but would welcome any languages (bar Spanish, which is well covered). The process is quite easy, Michael writes: "We have some great technology that can caption almost automatically, and the karaoke format is unique on the net. If you might be able to help please send an email to <info@captionedmediaforobama.com>"

(ii) Activity Two: Global Supporters Call US Voters and Politicians on the Phone to Explain Global Support for Obama

During the primaries fight, international supporters placed call to undecided superdelegates when Obama was leading by at least 150 delegates, he only needed to win 30% of the vote in the remaining primaries to maintain his lead in the popular vote. The only way he could lose the nomination is if the 800 or so superdelegates go against the popular vote. However, the stronger Obama's support in the remaining primaries, the less likely it was that the Superdelegates would throw him under the bus. Global opinion itself was a factor many Superdelegates might bore in mind. This is how it worked. The Obama campaign website enables volunteers to make campaign calls. All you have to do is decide which state or demographic group (students, women etc.) you would like to talk to, login and then start calling the numbers you are assigned! There is some general advice on making calls. Most used Skype and kept the cost low to the US from anywhere in the world. By this means, the global support communities creatively demonstrated the extent and reasons for Obama's global support.

The conversations followed these general guidelines:

Start by explaining who you are, and asking if they would be happy to talk, for example: "Hi, I'm Justin from London, England, Paris, Lagos, and I'm part of an international movement supporting Senator Obama. I can't vote in this election, but if you have a few minutes I'd love to talk to you about how a President Obama would improve America's standing in the world."

Be polite and sensitive. Many people find phone calls from strangers annoying and, while most people will have received quite a few calls about the elections, as non-Americans there is the need to be particularly careful not to offend potential voters.

Tell them a little about yourself and your country, explaining why the US elections have such an impact on your life and why you think Obama will help improve relations between America and your country (and the rest of the world).

Ask about their views on foreign policy. If you disagree strongly, try not to get into an argument, but rather stress the positives about Senator Obama.

You might compare Senator Obama to politicians in your country, and express your hope that if he becomes President it could inspire improvements in your political system.

Explain that Obama is the preferred candidate in every international poll, including polls in Japan, Britain, Germany, Brazil, South Africa, France, Iraq . . . You could point out that in Canada and Britain—America's closest allies—Obama is not only the overall favorite candidate, but also the favorite candidate among conservatives, demonstrating his ability to cross partisan divides.

Mention your favorite stories and testimonies from section 3.4 of this book, for example the Pastor in Holland who says Obama's candidacy has dramatically reversed anti-American feeling among the Muslim immigrant community.

If they are particularly interested in world opinion, point them to this website (TheWorldWantsObama.org) for more information.

Try to end on a positive note, making sure you have mentioned some of the things you admire about America and Americans; the "Two Americas" article by Israeli peace activist Uri Averny makes the point well: "there are two Americas . . . the America of Hiroshima and McCarthy, and the other America, the America of the Declaration of Independence, of Lincoln, Wilson and Roosevelt. In these terms, George Bush belongs to the first. Obama, his opposite in almost every respect, represents the second."

(iii) Activity Three: Submit a "Dear American Voter . . . Video" to LinkTV

LinkTV, a non-profit TV channel in the US and online, is inviting people around the world to submit short videos sharing their views about the election.

This includes making videos that tell how you would vote, and why. Even better, don't just tell them, show them: How have U.S. policies already changed the place where you live? What about the lives of your friends and family?"

There are already 25 videos on this initiative. Supporters are encouraged to get out their webcams and record their messages! Make them short, polite and positive—explain which of Obama's characteristics and policies particularly appeal to you and your hopes for how America under his leadership might act and how it will be perceived in your country.

(iv) Activity Four: Bridges

The Obama Bridge Project is a fantastic initiative by international Obama supporters and Americans living abroad. The initiator, Meredith Wheeler in France, explains the rationale and invites everyone to join an existing photo being planned in his country, or to arrange one himself! The project is gathering photographs and videos of Obama supporters around the world, posing at, on or under famous or scenic bridges, displaying Obama banners—the bridge being an ideal symbol of the Obama candidacy. Bridges unite two banks, spans chasms, gaps and troubled water, and bring together opposing sides. We plan to gather these photographs together and make a powerful YouTube video and show it at the Democratic National convention in August. When possible, we encourage a video record of the event too, with a group "Yes, We Can" moment! Please get involved—YES WE SPAN! (forgive the pun!) There have been photos of this project on Flickr photos and Youtube videos from in Austria, Lebanon, Turkey, Britain, Ireland, Canada and many more countries.

(v) Activity Five: Suggest Policies to the Obama Campaign

The Obama campaign is inviting policy suggestions. "The best, most comprehensive plan for change in your country will include your ideas and your feedback. America needs a president with a mandate from the people, and everyone deserves a voice in shaping our next president's agenda." In this, the global support interprets "everyone" as including non-Americans affected by US policies. So everyone with some knowledge and expertise is providing some sensible ideas for improving US foreign policy related to his country, or in general, can submit them here: *http://my.barackobama. com/*page/s/mypolicy. You can also write a few paragraphs to the Campaign explaining why you support Senator Obama: http://my.barackobama. com/page/s/aafostory

(vi) Activity Six: Avaaz.org. Signing of a Global Petition as an Expression of Solidarity to Senator Obama

Avaaz.org, the global advocacy group, which gives expression to global public opinion on issues ranging from climate change to Darfur, is inviting us to send messages to Senator Obama. They write: The world can't vote in the US elections, nor will it help to preach to those who can. But Americans themselves say they want their next President to be someone who is respected around the world, so our voice counts this time—and as Obama tours the world, our best chance to be heard may be now. We're running this global petition as a gesture of worldwide friendship and solidarity with Obama. We will deliver this petition to the Obama campaign, the US media, and the blogosphere to show that his message of change inspires global respect, and to emphasise those issues on which his boldness is most needed:

People everywhere in the world are invited to Sign a petition and send a personal message and deliver right on the website. The sample message should go this way:

> "Senator Obama, we send you this gesture of respect and sign of hope from all around the world. Let's work together to stop climate change, protect human rights and prevent war, and help make the US a responsible and respected member of the global community again."

In trying to cover Obama's international appeal, the US Media has started to pick up stories of how popular Senator Obama is around the world. The New York Times (42) covered the Bridges for Obama photo campaign (which staged photos in Tokyo, Kiev and Sao Paulo recently, and the Washington Post covers it on it's campaign trail blog (43) this way: "For many people in the international community, Obama represents the opportunity of the U.S. to lead by example and inspiring countries to take action, instead of bullying them into submission. It is one of the reasons why Obama won a landslide victory among Democrats abroad, and why diplomats from throughout the world tend to speak so positively about Obama." Another American responds: "If the rest of the world sees Obama in a more positive light . . . . considering our horrific international image (thanks to George Bush), obviously this would greatly improve our image world-wide. After all, we are NOT an island and cannot exist without the alliance of other countries. We have to stop thinking that we are isolated and small . . . it is this very notion that got us into this mess in the first place."

3.3   Can World Support Hurt Obama?

Israeli journalist Shmuel Rosner (44) has an interesting article in Slate "Does the world's enthusiasm for Barack Obama hurt him? He claims that President Obama would inevitably disappoint the world. He alludes that: "some of the premises on which his popularity rests would prove to be valid: He might handle Guantanamo better, pay more attention to global warming, speak more softly, and hide the stick—for a while." However he contends that: "Doing those things would eventually make it more difficult for him to operate in the world of power politics . . . Obama would suffer the consequences of high expectations. He would be trapped between the desire to preserve his high standing in the world and the need to act in ways that would erode that standing."

This issue is complex and hard to predict, but important. Most of the global voices we hear recognize that President Obama will face difficult choices and they will not agree with everything he does. Indeed some of his current policies—for example his lean towards Israel (although he still ranks lowest in Rosner's weekly poll of Israeli opinion-formers)—are already unpopular internationally. Most people are not expecting a Messiah, but rather a human being, limited in many ways by Congress and other factors, but nonetheless driven by strong values, a willingness to listen, and the courage to act. Obama would certainly disappoint the most exaggerated expectations, but if American voters reject him, we fear that global disappointment and cynicism towards America will increase even more.

Just as the international supporters organizing contributed to Obama's victory in primaries, a continued support will produce an ultimate victory in the November general elections.

3.4   And There are Reports of How Obama is Already Improving America's Image Abroad!

After steady fall throughout George Bush's term in office, global perspectives about America are growing (slightly) more positive. The annual attitudes poll commissioned by the BBC **(45)** of over 17,000 people in 35 countries shows an improvement in US ratings in 11 countries and a fall in only 3. Overall 35% of people said the US had a positive influence in the world, compared with 31% a year ago; the percentage that discerned a negative influence fell from 52% from 47%.

"Analysts involved in the survey said a number of factors were at play. The US presidential primaries have showcased a less ideological, more approachable America and at the very least raised hopes of a more conciliatory approach to foreign policy once President Bush steps down. "The image of the US is already being influenced by the prospect of one of the candidates becoming president," says Dr. Kull of PIPA. "All three talk more about multi-lateralism and cooperation; all express concern about the US image in the world; all express substantial concern about climate change and signal readiness to take action on that front."

While it is certainly true that all three candidates are viewed in a better light than Bush, the evidence gathered by The World Wants Obama Coalition (polls for example) show that Obama is by far the most egalitarian, and therefore can be given most of the credit for the improvement in the US' image abroad. It will be interesting to see the results of the BBC attitudes poll next year if it happens a few months after President Obama's inauguration. Our prediction is that such a poll would show a very large improvement in attitudes to the US.

Obama is already changing the world. From Holland, Obama's candidacy has reversed anti-Americanism among immigrants in Holland. A powerful example of the way Senator Obama is changing international attitudes towards America comes from Reverend Axel, **(46)** a German who ministers to a church in Amsterdam, Holland. He's only visited the US as a child and has two American cousins, but his experiences of interfaith dialogue with Muslim immigrants in Amsterdam has given him a dramatic impression of Obama's candidacy. When uncommitted Superdelegate Debra Kozikowski asked people to convince her which candidate to support with her vote, Axel explained:

"I live in a very multicultural neighborhood. Within 500m around the church I work in, there is a synagogue, a small Buddhist shrine, a Hindu temple and three mosques . . . more than 80 nationalities are represented in my district. The majority of the young people in my neighborhood are children of immigrants from Muslim countries: Morocco, Pakistan, Iran, Turkey, Egypt and a few others . . . Since 9/11, my neighborhood has seen quite a big share of Anti-Americanism: demonstrations, lots of graffiti, the burning of the American flag . . . my cousin Scott from Pennsylvania . . . got beaten up by a gang, because of his American accent. Other American friends of mine, who lived a couple of streets away, felt forced to move to another area of town which was safer for them. Shops selling US products closed down after their windows were thrown in several times. Even in my work, Anti-Americanism flared up: In an effort to reach out to the neighborhood and to bridge religious divides, my parish, in corporation with one of the more open mosques in the area started a group called 'Dialogue' in 2003 which every week attracts about 50 people from all backgrounds with at least 50% being Muslim. Regularly after big political events in the US (with Bush's reelection having the worst effect) or in the Middle East, discussions in this group quickly turn fiercely political and often viciously Anti-American. I must confess, although some people were merely regurgitating talking points of radical propagandists, over the years, I could also feel genuine pain of feeling discriminated against. And although often, people wrongly expanded their anger towards the ignorance and intolerance of the Bush administration to all things American, I often could understand or even share their dislike of American politics."

"In a nutshell, I support Barrack Obama because of what his candidacy has changed in the mindset of many of these ordinary Muslims in this inter-religious group which I moderate together with the local Imam. Shortly after Iowa, Obama was first mentioned by Mustafa, an elderly man, who immigrated here from Morocco and never before had said anything nearly positive about America. In fact, he quite shocked me, as he interrupted Bahaar, a young Muslim of Pakistani descent, who had just started a monologue about the devilish American culture and how he wanted to kill Bush, the crusader. Mustafa stood up and told him: "Well you better hurry up, then: Bush is gone by the end of this year, and you know, I think, the next President will be much, much better: He was against invading Iraq and has lived in Indonesia when he was young!" This totally changed the tone of the discussion that night and in fact, in all meetings of our group 'Dialogue' since then, we hardly have discussed anything else except Obama's rise, his stance on foreign policy, his life story, what it says about American culture and what impact it may have on how the world sees America. I have to say, that personally, after moderating this group for five years now, I'm simply overwhelmed about the impact of Obama on ordinary Muslims! The last meetings were by far the most constructive and healing we have had so far. Lots of the participants are reviewing their prejudices against America or are now at least able to differentiate between American politics and Americans. The day before yesterday, at our last meeting, hot-headed Bahaar summed it up very well: "Well, I guess if Americans vote for someone like him . . . they can't be all that bad!" For him, this is a radical turn of 180 degrees!!!"

"So you see, it's amazing, what only Obama's run has created over here: Lots of people in my neighborhood, who until now, simply believed what the propagandists told them about American politics, got active and looked up in-depth information about the US primaries and about Obama. Often also, he got covered on Al-Jazeera and other Arab TV networks and every time, I witness the effect in my neighborhood. Yesterday, I went out shopping and suddenly spotted a poster of the Obama-campaign in the window of my grocery-dealer, who immigrated to Holland from Iran. He told me that he saw him on television and got so excited that he downloaded the poster from the internet and put it up. He would love him to become president, because with him, "finally, someone will talk to the idiot running my country!" And get this: A couple of days ago, my 73 year-old neighbor Mohammed who came here from Egypt asked me to look up "on the computer", how he can donate 5 USD to Obama's campaign, because he would love an American president who understands ordinary people in Muslim countries. He was very disappointed when I told him that only US citizens can donate. He vowed, however, to pray for Obama later at the mosque!"

"As far as I'm concerned: I cannot underestimate, how much the election of Barrack Obama for next President of the USA would improve the perception of America by ordinary people around the world and especially by people living in developing and/or Muslim countries. And quite frankly, after two disastrous Bush-administrations, I can hardly wait!!! I sincerely hope, that this little story of mine can help you decide who to support on the convention of the Democratic Party!"

References

1. http://www.theworldwantsobama.org
2. http://www.barackobama.com/learn/meet_barack.php
3. http://www.theworldwantsobama.org/2008_02_0 1_archive.html
4. Andrew Sullivan. The rebranding of America. The Daily Disk. 24 Apr 2007. http://andrewsullivan.theatlantic.com/the_daily_dish/2007/04/the_rebranding_.html
5. Byron York. http://thehill.com/byron-york/obama-for-president-of-the-world-2008-06-19.html
6. Andrew Sullivan. The rebranding of America. The Daily Disk. 24 Apr 2007. http://andrewsullivan.theatlantic.com/the_daily_dish/2007/04/the_rebranding_.html
7. http://www.theworldwantsobama.org/2008/06/obama-comes-top-in-poll-of-business.html
8. http://www.theworldwantsobama.org/2008_03_01_archive.html
9. http://www.theworldwantsobama.org/2008_07_01_archive.html
10. http://www.theworldwantsobama.org/2008_06_01_archive.html
11. http://www.theworldwantsobama.org/2008_05_01_archive.html
12. http://www.theworldwantsobama.org/2008_03_01_archive.html
13. http://www.theworldwantsobama.org/2008_04_01_archive.html
14. http://www.theworldwantsobama.org/2008_04_01_archive.html
15. http://www.theworldwantsobama.org/2008_06_01_archive.html
16. http://www.theworldwantsobama.org/2008_03_01_archive.html
17. http://www.theworldwantsobama.org/2008_03_01_ archive.html
18. http://www.theworldwantsobama.org/2008_02_01_archive.html
19. http://www.theworldwantsobama.org/2008_02_01_archive.html
20. http://www.theworldwantsobama.org/2008_02_01_archive.html
21. http://www.theworldwantsobama.org/2008_04_01_archive.html
22. http://www.theworldwantsobama.org/2008_01_01_archive.html

23. http://www.theworldwantsobama.org/2008_02_01_archive.html
24. http://www.theworldwantsobama.org/2008_02_01_archive.html
25. http://www.theworldwantsobama.org/2008_02_01_archive.html
26. http://www.theworldwantsobama.org/2008_04_01_archive.html
27. http://www.theworldwantsobama.org/2008_02_01_archive.html
28. http://www.theworldwantsobama.org/2008_04_01_archive.html
29. http://www.theworldwantsobama.org/2008_01_01_ archive.html.
30. http://www.theworldwantsobama.org/2008_03_01_archive.html
31. http://www.theworldwantsobama.org/2008_03_01_archive.html
32. http://www.theworldwantsobama.org/2008_03_01_archive.html
33. http://www.theworldwantsobama.org/2008_04_01_archive.html
34. http://www.theworldwantsobama.org/2008_03_01_archive.html
35. http://www.theworldwantsobama.org/2008_03_01_archive.html
36. http://www.theworldwantsobama.org/2008_04_01_archive.html
37. http://www.theworldwantsobama.org/2008_04_01_archive.html
38. http://www.washingtonpost.com/wp-dyn/content/story/2008/07/25/
    ST2008072502074.html
39. http://www.theworldwantsobama.org/2008_02_01_archive.html
40. http://www.theworldwantsobama.org/2008_05_01_archive.html
41. http://www.theworldwantsobama.org/2008_07_01_archive.html
42. http://www.theworldwantsobama.org/2008_05_01_archive.html
43. http://www.theworldwantsobama.org/2008_05_01_archive.html
44. http://www.theworldwantsobama.org/2008_04_01 archive.html
45. http://www.theworldwantsobama.org/2008_04_01_archive.html
46. http://www.theworldwantsobama.org/2008_04_01_archive.html

www.ingramcontent.com/pod-product-compliance
Lightning Source LLC
Chambersburg PA
CBHW031745290526
45784CB00017B/2541